The Way of the Cross

Travelling with Jesus

David Adam

with illustrations by
Melody-Anne Lee

kevin
mayhew

First published in Great Britain in 2008 by Kevin Mayhew Ltd
Buxhall, Stowmarket, Suffolk IP14 3BW
Tel: +44 (0) 1449 737978 Fax: +44 (0) 1449 737834
E-mail: info@kevinmayhewltd.com

www.kevinmayhew.com

9 8 7 6 5 4 3 2 1 0

ISBN 978 1 84867 081 5
Catalogue No. 1501139

Illustrations and design by Melody-Anne Lee
Edited by Katherine Laidler
Typeset by Richard Weaver

Printed and bound in Great Britain

Contents

Foreword

The Way of the Cross, often called the Stations of the Cross, is found in the Catholic, Anglican and Lutheran traditions. It may be used at any time of the year but especially on Fridays in Lent and on Good Friday. It makes a good personal devotion and can be used for meditation using just one or two stations a day or spending time to travel to all of the stations.

The Stations of the Cross began in Jerusalem on the Via Dolorosa (the Sorrowful Way) where pilgrims sought to stop, pray and meditate at various places where tradition said certain events happened. Some of the stations had no basis in Scripture, though they could well have happened, and were used to illustrate the fullness of the saving acts. The non-Scriptural stations are the three falls of Jesus, Jesus meeting his mother, and Veronica wiping his face. The stations were found in artwork or carvings all over Europe by the fifteenth century. Possibly the devotion arose especially for pilgrims who could not hope to travel to Jerusalem. The Stations of the Cross have provided a visual devotion for countless Christians. The number of stations has varied – some would restrict them to the biblically based stations – but usually there are now the fourteen stations.

How to pray the Stations

Above all, it must be remembered that the stations are an act of pilgrimage: this is not an intellectual exercise but an act of devotion. The heart and the imagination have to be able to come into play. The stations are a journey in awareness not only of historical events but of 'the lamb that was slain before the foundation of the world' (Revelation 13:8); awareness of the presence of the Lord in our lives, in our suffering and in suffering humanity. The Way of the Cross travels through our world and is present wherever someone is betrayed by a kiss or deserted by loved ones; wherever anyone suffers injustice or enters into darkness. Christ is found with the poor and the powerless, with the scorned and rejected. In the midst of all life the Lord is there. The Way of the Cross is a journey with our Lord. It is a journey into the love of God as revealed in his Son Jesus Christ. The crucified one knows our troubles and he is with us always.

We are faced with wonder and mystery. God comes down: the Creator is in the hands of his creation. The Maker of the world is edged out of the world, out of the city, out of lives and on to the cross. He who came to set us free is fixed by nails, he who came to give life is put to death. What is the meaning of all of this? We are to learn that love is his meaning. He comes to us out of love, gives himself in love and love holds him on the cross. The best preparation for us to enter into this wonder and mystery is silence and stillness. We stand before events that the mind can hardly grasp, but the heart can feel. Do not rush the stations; take your time with each one and enter into stillness – stations are where you stop for a while. Pause in the presence and let the power and love of God enfold you, and give your love to him.

Begin the stations with a personal prayer that centres on the presence and love of God. Be still and quiet and give your love to him.

> In the saving power of God, Father,
> Son and Holy Spirit.

> Blessed are you Lord God of our salvation,
> in your love for us
> you gave us your Son to be our Redeemer.
> As I walk the way of the cross,
> may I walk with Christ our Lord
> and know his great love for me.
> As he gave himself for me,
> help me to give my life to you,
> blessed Father, Son and Holy Spirit.

After each station is named say:

> I adore you, O Christ, and I bless you,
> **because by your holy cross**
> **you have redeemed the world.**

At the end of each station let there be a silence and then, before moving on to the next station, say:

> Lord Jesus Christ, who by your cross and passion have redeemed us,
> **save and help us, I humbly beseech you, O Lord.**

First station
Jesus is condemned to death

He was despised and rejected by others; a man of suffering and acquainted with infirmity . . . Surely he has borne our infirmities and carried our diseases . . . He was wounded for our transgressions, crushed for our iniquities; upon him was the punishment that made us whole, and by his bruises we are healed. All we like sheep have gone astray; we have all turned to our own way, and the Lord has laid on him the iniquity of us all. He was oppressed, and he was afflicted, yet he did not open his mouth; like a lamb that is led to the slaughter, and like a sheep that before its shearers is silent, so he did not open his mouth.

Isaiah 53:3-7

The powers of this world are determined
    to be rid of Jesus.
He challenges their way of life,
their power structures,
their luxury whilst others starve,
their insensitivity towards their fellows,
and for this he is condemned.

The church people are not comfortable with him.
He talks about their dedication.
He questions their lack of mission.
He wants them to love as God loves,
and for this he is condemned.

He came in love and they vent their hatred upon him.
He came to enrich their lives and they strip him and
    leave him bare.
He came to give life and they condemn him to death.
He sought to set them free and they fix him to a cross
    of wood.

Jesus, help me to accept you as my Lord and my God.
Increase my sensitivity to your presence in others:
help me to know that as I do it to the least of all
I do it to you.

Second station
Jesus receives the cross

'The Son of Man must undergo great suffering, and be rejected by the elders, chief priests and scribes, and be killed, and on the third day be raised.' Then he said to them all, 'If any want to become my followers, let them deny themselves and take up their cross daily and follow me. For those who want to save their life will lose it, and those who lose their life for my sake will save it. What does it profit them if they gain the whole world, but lose or forfeit themselves?'

Luke 9:22-25

Here is the cross.
Take it as if it is yours, as if you deserved it.
Take upon you the injustice, the cruelty
    and the hatred of the world.
Take upon you all the pain and sorrow.
Lord, you give yourself in love –
let me not give a cross to you.

Jesus, I remember all who are forced to accept
    suffering as their daily lot,
all who are betrayed by loved ones,
all deserted by their friends,
all who are very much left alone.
In you may they find hope.

Third station
Jesus falls for the first time

Cursed is the ground because of you; in toil you shall eat of it all the days of your life; thorns and thistles it shall bring forth for you; and you shall eat the plants of the field. By the sweat of your face you shall eat bread until you return to the ground, for out of it you were taken; you are dust, and to dust you shall return.

Genesis 3:17-19

The Son of Man is weakened;
a heart is breaking with love.
He came down to lift us up,
and now he descends to the dust.
God and dust mix together.
He humbled himself unto death,
even death on the cross.
Now he crawls in the dust – see how the dust clings
    to him as he arises!
He comes down to the lowest level to raise us up.

Lord Jesus, many are your humiliations:
born in a stable, taken as a refugee,
scorned and rejected, betrayed with a kiss,
denied by a friend, deserted by disciples,
brought down to the dust.
I remember before you
all who suffer humiliation and all who are brought low.

Fourth station
Jesus is met by his mother

Then Simeon blessed them and said to his mother Mary, 'This child is destined for the falling and the rising of many in Israel, and to be a sign that will be opposed so that the inner thoughts of many will be revealed – and a sword will pierce your own soul too.'

Luke 2:34, 35

Mary ought not to have come, but love drew her to him.
This would cost her much pain and sorrow, agony
   and awful memories.
Why should this happen to him, to her?
What had either done to deserve this?
There seemed to be no answer.

Pain is not a private thing; it is shared by loved ones.
If one suffers, all suffer.
Mary experiences the sword that was to pierce
   her heart.

Lord, I fear that if I love you,
I will be asked to walk the way of the cross.
If I give you my heart,
it will be pierced with the sorrows of the world.

Fifth station
Simon of Cyrene is compelled to carry the cross

They compelled a passer-by, who was coming in from the country, to carry his cross; it was Simon of Cyrene, the father of Alexander and Rufus. Then they brought Jesus to the place called Golgotha (which means the place of a skull).

Mark 15:21, 22

Simon is an African, as Cyrene was what is now Libya.
He had no intentions of doing anything.
He was entering the city from the country.
He is forced to carry the cross.
That day he learnt something that would change him –
for we are told his sons are known by the Church.
Military rule forces its will on people.
People are still compelled to do awful things.
The cross is to be borne in our helping of the least,
in the hungry,
the refugee,
the homeless,
the outcasts.
The Lord calls us to bear one another's burdens.

Lord, as you have given your life for me,
help me to give myself to others
and to you.

Sixth station
Veronica wipes the face of Jesus

Hear, O Lord, when I cry aloud,
be gracious to me and answer me!
'Come,' my heart says, 'seek his face!'
Your face, Lord, do I seek.
Do not hide your face from me.

Psalm 27:7-9

Jesus had been badly beaten.
His face is covered with sweat, dust and blood.
He is not a pretty sight.
One in the crowd is moved by his suffering.
She comes forward and stands out from the crowd.
She disregards the danger and the hostility;
she acts on impulse out of love.
It is said that the face of Jesus was captured on the
    cloth she used to wipe his face.
She would keep this image in her heart.
She would remember this face, a face like any other face,
but she had looked into the eyes of God.
The face of God is scarred by thorns,
bloodied by violence.

Lord, how often I defile your image
and mar your likeness.
Forgive me and help me to reveal you to others.

Seventh station
Jesus falls a second time

My soul clings to the dust;
revive me according to your word.
My soul melts away for sorrow;
strengthen me according to your word.
Let your steadfast love come to me, O Lord,
your salvation according to your promise.
Then shall I have an answer for those who taunt me,
for I trust in your word.

Psalm 119:25, 28, 41, 42

Lord, do you never give up?
You are down again –
and I know it will not be for the last time.
How long must you suffer?
How long can your creation defile and degrade you?
Once again you bite the dust for us
and for our salvation.
Dust and divinity mingling together:
dust rising with you when you arise.

Lord, when I attach myself to you, I arise,
for with you is life and life eternal.

Eighth station
Jesus meets the women of Jerusalem

A great number of people followed him, and among them were women who were beating their breasts and wailing for him. But Jesus turned to them and said, 'Daughters of Jerusalem, do not weep for me, but weep for yourselves and for your children. For the days are surely coming when they will say, "Blessed are the barren, and the wombs that never bore, and the breasts that never nursed." Then they will begin to say to the mountains, "Fall on us"; and to the hills, "Cover us." For if they do this when the wood is green, what will happen when it is dry?'

Luke 23:27-31

Only the hardened and the toughest of people would
    not be moved,
but many regimes brutalise people.
Some women are openly weeping for Jesus;
    their hearts are stirred.
The mothers know a mother's heart must be breaking.
It causes tears to flow.
The sorrow of women for their children
    is a great sorrow.
Jesus accepts their sympathy – but with a warning.
More than tears are needed to change the world.
If they can do this to a just man,
what will they do to others?
If this can be done to the Son of God,
then no one is safe.

Lord, I come to you in sorrow
for the suffering peoples of the world.
Give me the courage and willpower to help where I can.

Ninth station
Jesus falls the third time

Christ Jesus who, though he was in the form of God,
did not regard equality with God
as something to be exploited,
but emptied himself,
taking the form of a slave,
being born in human likeness.
And being found in human form,
he humbled himself
and became obedient to the point of death –
even death on a cross.

Philippians 2:6-8

There you go, down again. This is becoming a habit.
You seem to be attached to the dust.
This time it looks as if this is it: are you still breathing?
Shall I count you out? I could count you out.
Are you already dead?
How long do you want to lie there: three days or more?
Death is not far away – but you rise again.

Lord Jesus, as the dust clings to you as you rise,
may I hold fast to you and to your saving power.

Tenth station
Jesus is stripped of his garments

My God, my God, why have you forsaken me?
Why are you so far from helping me,
from the words of my groaning?
I am poured out like water,
and all my bones are out of joint;
my heart is like wax;
it is melted within my breast;
my mouth is dried up like a potsherd,
and my tongue sticks to my jaws;
you lay me in the dust of death.
For dogs are all around me;
a company of evildoers encircles me.

My hands and feet have shrivelled;
I can count all my bones.
They stare and gloat over me;
they divide my clothes among themselves,
and for my clothing they cast lots.
But you, O Lord, do not be far away!
O my help, come quickly to my aid!

Psalm 22:1, 14-18

They have taken all from you.
Now they gamble for the robe your mother gave you.
They take away your dignity and leave you exposed.
They strip you of your humanity
and will take away your life.
There is no Transfiguration, no white robes,
only bareness;
nothing to shield you from the cross or from mockery.
You are defenceless or so it seems.
Yet in love you allow all this for us.

Lord, strip from me all false pride;
strip away all self-trust;
take away all that keeps me from you.
I remember before you all who are laid bare,
all who have nothing and are counted as nothing.

Eleventh station
Jesus is nailed to the cross

So they took Jesus; and carrying the cross by himself, he went out to what is called The Place of the Skull, which in Hebrew is called Golgotha. There they crucified him, and with him two others, one on either side, with Jesus between them. Pilate also had an inscription written and put on the cross. It read, 'Jesus of Nazareth, the King of the Jews.' Many of the Jews read this inscription, because the place where Jesus was crucified was near the city; and it was written in Hebrew, in Latin and in Greek.

John 19:16b-20

Jesus who came to set them free is fixed . . .
to a cross of wood.
Listen to the sound of the nails.
Iron on iron, iron into wood, all resound.
Human flesh does not make much sound,
neither does the Son of Man.
Here is planned cruelty and indignity.
Jesus is hung like a picture – but not a pretty sight.
Arms are stretched out as if to welcome in an embrace.
This is the cost of your love, of the love of God.
The Christ is poured out for us and for our salvation.

Lord, as you open your arms to welcome me,
let me remember the cost.
By your agony and loneliness,
support me in my troubles.
By your life laid down,
lift me up and bring me to life eternal.

Twelfth station
Jesus dies upon the cross

When it was noon, darkness came over the whole land until three in the afternoon. At three o'clock Jesus cried out with a loud voice, 'Eloi, Eloi, lema sabachthani?' which means, 'My God, my God, why have you forsaken me?' When some of the bystanders heard it, they said, 'Listen, he is calling for Elijah.' And someone ran, filled a sponge with sour wine, put it on a stick, and gave it to him to drink, saying, 'Wait, let us see whether Elijah will come to take him down.' Then Jesus gave a loud cry and breathed his last.

Mark 15:33-37

Can it be that God suffers for me?
Can it be that God dies for me?
The Christ has paid the extreme price of love:
he has laid down his life for us;
through him the darkness is banished.
He has served his Father faithfully even to death,
and in death he has become our Redeemer.
There is no greater love than this.

Lord Christ, my Redeemer,
as you give yourself for me and to me,
help me to give myself to you.

Jesus is taken down from the cross

When his parents saw him they were astonished; and his mother said to him, 'Child, why have you treated us like this? Look, your father and I have been searching for you in great anxiety.' He said to them, 'Why were you searching for me? Did you not know that I must be in my Father's house?'

Luke 2:48, 49

Once again Jesus returns to his mother's lap.
But there is no joy here: the body is broken
    and disfigured.
A sword pierces her own heart.
How long is it since he was last in her arms?
This is a far cry from Bethlehem and Nazareth:
there was so much promise;
it seemed the whole world would follow him.
Now Jesus, her son, is dead.
He came to his own but his own received him not.
The creature has sought to kill the Creator.
What hells are let loose on the world?

Lord Christ,
I remember all who are facing death
or the death of a loved one.
I pray for all who have been killed
through violence or accidents.
Lord, in your death may I find hope.

Fourteenth station
Jesus is laid in the tomb

When evening had come, and since it was the day of Preparation, that is, the day before the Sabbath, Joseph of Arimathea, a respected member of the council, who was also himself waiting expectantly for the kingdom of God, went boldly to Pilate and asked for the body of Jesus. Then Pilate wondered if he were already dead; and summoning the centurion, he asked him whether he had been dead for some time. When he learned from the centurion that he was dead, he granted the body to Joseph. Then Joseph bought a linen cloth, and taking down the body, wrapped it in the linen cloth, and laid it in a tomb that had been hewn out of the rock. He then rolled a stone against the door of the tomb. Mary Magdalene and Mary the mother of Joses saw where the body was laid.

Mark 15:42-47

As the sun goes down, the Christ is buried
    in a borrowed grave.
After all the pain and agony he looks at rest:
the whiteness of the linen cloth
    helps to hide the wounds and scars.
He lies here like a seed buried in the earth.
This is the winter of the world:
all who love him are left numbed and cold,
exhausted and empty.
At least he has passed beyond it all.

Lord Jesus, come into our darkness,
into our lives sealed against feeling,
into our many deaths.
Help me to know that you are beyond the grave
and beckon me to glory.